TAX *Agenda*
FOR
ENTREPRENEURS

CRYSTAL COLÓN

EDITED AND DESIGNED BY AMTUL BATOOL
OF GOLDEN GOOSE STUDIO

As an auditor and small business owner, I know first-hand how daunting record keeping and taxes can be. Luckily for me, I have a background in taxes. I have been dealing with tax in one way or another since I was 16 years old. Whether I was filing or running tape for my uncle in his accounting office, I was soaking up accounting and tax information like a sponge.

I want to share some of the information I have learned over the years with small business owners like you. You may be a wife, husband, mother or father with many other things you need to take care of besides taxes. You are busy running a business. You don't have time to be stressing out at the beginning of the year because you didn't organize your finances the year before. You need a tax planner, one that can be of use to you throughout the year as you gather all the information you need in one place to hand off to your tax preparer at year's end.

Use this tax planner regularly to track your income and expenses and plan the quarterly and monthly goals for your business. Whether you want to increase profit, decrease a particular expense, update your website, or maybe even develop a new product or service by a certain time, use this planner to get organized and make it happen!

I am available to answer any questions you may have. Thank you for selecting this awesome resource for your tax planning purposes. I pray your business is blessed abundantly!

With Love,

IMPORTANT INFO

I don't know about you, but I frequently need this information, and I ALWAYS end up having to search through emails and other files on my computer to find what I need. That's why I wanted to have a central location for the basic information we all need to run our businesses. Hope this helps!

NAME: _____

BUSINESS NAME: _____

EIN: _____

BUSINESS WEBSITE: _____

ACCOUNTANT NAME: _____

ACCOUNTANT PHONE NUMBER: _____

ATTORNEY NAME: _____

ATTORNEY PHONE NUMBER: _____

BANK NAME: _____

BANKER PHONE NUMBER: _____

BANK ACCOUNT NUMBER: _____

BANK ROUTING NUMBER: _____

The following maybe applicable to you, as well:

STATE EIN: _____

SALES TAX NUMBER: _____

STATE TAX WEBSITE USER ID: _____
(for filing taxes electronically such as franchise tax or sales taxes)

QUARTER 1 GOALS

Use this sheet to plan goals for the quarter. Whether its launching a new product or improving the way you do business, whatever your goals are for the quarter, jot them down here and check them off when you have accomplished the goal. Simple!

GROSS INCOME

Report ALL income you receive REGARDLESS of whether or not you receive an information return (W2, 1099, etc.) You are still liable for a correct reporting of income. So do your part to keep track of income you receive. An easy way to do this is to open a separate business bank account. Deposit ALL income into that account. Then withdraw funds from that account as needed. At years end you simply have to total your deposits to arrive at the correct income (assuming that said income DID NOT have withholding. If that income had withholding, you need to determine the GROSS amount).

IMPORTANT NOTES & IDEAS

Use this calendar to record business appointments, jot down mileage, and keep track of business meals and other noteworthy items you may need to reference through the year.

_____ (MONTH) _____ (YEAR)

SUNDAY	MONDAY	TUESDAY	WEDNESDAY	THURSDAY	FRIDAY	SATURDAY

Notes

Goals

MONTHLY BUSINESS INCOME & EXPENSES

Use the following table to budget and record actual expenses for your business. The items listed below are the common expenses found on business tax forms. At years end, calculate the totals and hand to your accountant (with receipts for back up of course).

INCOME	PROJECTED	ACTUAL
MONTH #1		

EXPENSES	PROJECTED	ACTUAL
ADVERTISING		
CAR & TRUCK		
COMMISSIONS & FEES		
CONTRACT LABOR		
DEPLETION		
DEPRECIATION		
EMPLOYEE BENEFIT PLANS		
INSURANCE		
MORTGAGE		
LEGAL & PROFESSIONAL FEES		
OFFICE EXPENSES RENSIONS		
RENT OR LEASE (VEHICLES)		
RENT OR LEASE (OTHER BUSINESS PROPERTY)		
REPAIRS & MAINTENANCE		
SUPPLIES		
TAXES & LICENSES		
TRAVEL		
MEALS & ENTERTAINMENT		
UTILITIES		
WAGES		
OTHER EXPENSES		
TOTAL		

BUSINESS USE OF HOME

To deduct expenses for business use of home you must:

» use part of your home for your FOR PROFIT trade or business

» use the SPECIFIC space EXCLUSIVELY for business

You are a blogger using a den in your home to write blog posts and take pictures for social media. Your family also uses the den for entertainment and family activities. The den is not used exclusively for your business, therefore, you cannot claim a deduction for the business use of that space.

IMPORTANT NOTES & IDEAS

Use this calendar to record business appointments, jot down mileage, and keep track of business meals and other noteworthy items you may need to reference through the year.

_____ (MONTH) _____ (YEAR)

SUNDAY	MONDAY	TUESDAY	WEDNESDAY	THURSDAY	FRIDAY	SATURDAY

Notes

Goals

MONTHLY BUSINESS INCOME & EXPENSES

Use the following table to budget and record actual expenses for your business. The items listed below are the common expenses found on business tax forms. At years end, calculate the totals and hand to your accountant (with receipts for back up of course).

INCOME	PROJECTED	ACTUAL
MONTH #1		

EXPENSES	PROJECTED	ACTUAL
ADVERTISING		
CAR & TRUCK		
COMMISSIONS & FEES		
CONTRACT LABOR		
DEPLETION		
DEPRECIATION		
EMPLOYEE BENEFIT PLANS		
INSURANCE		
MORTGAGE		
LEGAL & PROFESSIONAL FEES		
OFFICE EXPENSES RENSIONS		
RENT OR LEASE (VEHICLES)		
RENT OR LEASE (OTHER BUSINESS PROPERTY)		
REPAIRS & MAINTENANCE		
SUPPLIES		
TAXES & LICENSES		
TRAVEL		
MEALS & ENTERTAINMENT		
UTILITIES		
WAGES		
OTHER EXPENSES		
TOTAL		

ESTIMATED TAXES

Estimated tax is paid on income that DID NOT have withholding or if your withholding is insufficient. This includes Self Employment (S/E) income among other types of income. Be sure to budget for taxes each month and set aside money so you won't be hit with a large tax bill that you don't have funds for.

Use **Form 1040-ES** to calculate and report Estimated Tax.

IMPORTANT NOTES & IDEAS

Use this calendar to record business appointments, jot down mileage, and keep track of business meals and other noteworthy items you may need to reference through the year.

_____ (MONTH) _____ (YEAR)

SUNDAY	MONDAY	TUESDAY	WEDNESDAY	THURSDAY	FRIDAY	SATURDAY

Notes

Goals

MONTHLY BUSINESS INCOME & EXPENSES

Use the following table to budget and record actual expenses for your business. The items listed below are the common expenses found on business tax forms. At years end, calculate the totals and hand to your accountant (with receipts for back up of course).

INCOME	PROJECTED	ACTUAL
MONTH #1		

EXPENSES	PROJECTED	ACTUAL
ADVERTISING		
CAR & TRUCK		
COMMISSIONS & FEES		
CONTRACT LABOR		
DEPLETION		
DEPRECIATION		
EMPLOYEE BENEFIT PLANS		
INSURANCE		
MORTGAGE		
LEGAL & PROFESSIONAL FEES		
OFFICE EXPENSES RENSIONS		
RENT OR LEASE (VEHICLES)		
RENT OR LEASE (OTHER BUSINESS PROPERTY)		.
REPAIRS & MAINTENANCE		
SUPPLIES		
TAXES & LICENSES		
TRAVEL		
MEALS & ENTERTAINMENT		
UTILITIES		
WAGES		
OTHER EXPENSES		
TOTAL		

QUARTER 2 GOALS

Use this sheet to plan goals for the quarter. Whether its launching a new product or improving the way you do business, whatever your goals are for the quarter, jot them down here and check them off when you have accomplished the goal. Simple!

FILING EXTENSION

Did you know that filing an extension on April 15 DOES NOT extend the time to *pay* tax? Taxes are due to be paid EVERY YEAR on April 15.

Use **Form 4868** to request an extension to file your tax return.

* If you don't pay the amount due by the due date, you will owe interest and may be charged penalties.

IMPORTANT NOTES & IDEAS

Use this calendar to record business appointments, jot down mileage, and keep track of business meals and other noteworthy items you may need to reference through the year.

_____ (MONTH) _____ (YEAR)

SUNDAY	MONDAY	TUESDAY	WEDNESDAY	THURSDAY	FRIDAY	SATURDAY

Notes

Goals

MONTHLY BUSINESS INCOME & EXPENSES

Use the following table to budget and record actual expenses for your business. The items listed below are the common expenses found on business tax forms. At years end, calculate the totals and hand to your accountant (with receipts for back up of course).

INCOME	PROJECTED	ACTUAL
MONTH #1		

EXPENSES	PROJECTED	ACTUAL
ADVERTISING		
CAR & TRUCK		
COMMISSIONS & FEES		
CONTRACT LABOR		
DEPLETION		
DEPRECIATION		
EMPLOYEE BENEFIT PLANS		
INSURANCE		
MORTGAGE		
LEGAL & PROFESSIONAL FEES		
OFFICE EXPENSES RENSIONS		
RENT OR LEASE (VEHICLES)		
RENT OR LEASE (OTHER BUSINESS PROPERTY)		
REPAIRS & MAINTENANCE		
SUPPLIES		
TAXES & LICENSES		
TRAVEL		
MEALS & ENTERTAINMENT		
UTILITIES		
WAGES		
OTHER EXPENSES		
TOTAL		

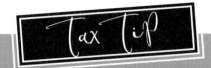

CAN I DEDUCT THIS?

You can deduct expenses that are ***ordinary and necessary***. Ordinary and necessary means expenses that are common, accepted, helpful and appropriate in your respective field or industry. These expenses can be deducted when you pay for them with cash. If, however, you are on the accrual basis, you will deduct these ordinary and necessary expenses when you incur the expense (i.e. when you enter into a contract and receive an invoice, even if said invoice has not yet been paid).

IMPORTANT NOTES & IDEAS

Use this calendar to record business appointments, jot down mileage, and keep track of business meals and other noteworthy items you may need to reference through the year.

_____ (MONTH)   _____ (YEAR)

SUNDAY	MONDAY	TUESDAY	WEDNESDAY	THURSDAY	FRIDAY	SATURDAY

Notes

Goals

MONTHLY BUSINESS INCOME & EXPENSES

Use the following table to budget and record actual expenses for your business. The items listed below are the common expenses found on business tax forms. At years end, calculate the totals and hand to your accountant (with receipts for back up of course).

INCOME	PROJECTED	ACTUAL
MONTH #1		

EXPENSES	PROJECTED	ACTUAL
ADVERTISING		
CAR & TRUCK		
COMMISSIONS & FEES		
CONTRACT LABOR		
DEPLETION		
DEPRECIATION		
EMPLOYEE BENEFIT PLANS		
INSURANCE		
MORTGAGE		
LEGAL & PROFESSIONAL FEES		
OFFICE EXPENSES RENSIONS		
RENT OR LEASE (VEHICLES)		
RENT OR LEASE (OTHER BUSINESS PROPERTY)		
REPAIRS & MAINTENANCE		
SUPPLIES		
TAXES & LICENSES		
TRAVEL		
MEALS & ENTERTAINMENT		
UTILITIES		
WAGES		
OTHER EXPENSES		
TOTAL		

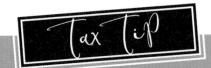

CAR & TRUCK EXPENSES

You should maintain a mileage log. If you aren't keen on writing all your mileage down each day, there are plenty of apps available to use. Another tip is to scan your business receipts, create a spreadsheet, and then use mapquest.com to calculate mileage.

* Scan receipts monthly or quarterly to reduce the stress and time of doing it all at once at the end of the year.

IMPORTANT NOTES & IDEAS

Use this calendar to record business appointments, jot down mileage, and keep track of business meals and other noteworthy items you may need to reference through the year.

_____ (MONTH)   _____ (YEAR)

SUNDAY	MONDAY	TUESDAY	WEDNESDAY	THURSDAY	FRIDAY	SATURDAY

Notes

Goals

MONTHLY BUSINESS INCOME & EXPENSES

Use the following table to budget and record actual expenses for your business. The items listed below are the common expenses found on business tax forms. At years end, calculate the totals and hand to your accountant (with receipts for back up of course).

INCOME	PROJECTED	ACTUAL
MONTH #1		

EXPENSES	PROJECTED	ACTUAL
ADVERTISING		
CAR & TRUCK		
COMMISSIONS & FEES		
CONTRACT LABOR		
DEPLETION		
DEPRECIATION		
EMPLOYEE BENEFIT PLANS		
INSURANCE		
MORTGAGE		
LEGAL & PROFESSIONAL FEES		
OFFICE EXPENSES RENSIONS		
RENT OR LEASE (VEHICLES)		
RENT OR LEASE (OTHER BUSINESS PROPERTY)		
REPAIRS & MAINTENANCE		
SUPPLIES		
TAXES & LICENSES		
TRAVEL		
MEALS & ENTERTAINMENT		
UTILITIES		
WAGES		
OTHER EXPENSES		
TOTAL		

QUARTER 3 GOALS

Use this sheet to plan goals for the quarter. Whether its launching a new product or improving the way you do business, whatever your goals are for the quarter, jot them down here and check them off when you have accomplished the goal. Simple!

- ☐ _____
- ☐ _____
- ☐ _____
- ☐ _____
- ☐ _____
- ☐ _____
- ☐ _____
- ☐ _____
- ☐ _____
- ☐ _____
- ☐ _____
- ☐ _____
- ☐ _____
- ☐ _____
- ☐ _____
- ☐ _____
- ☐ _____
- ☐ _____
- ☐ _____
- ☐ _____

MEALS & ENTERTAINMENT

Remember that meals & entertainment expenses are limited to 50% of ordinary and necessary business meals. Be sure to have a calendar documenting meetings over meals and some sort of proof of the business purpose. Instead of keeping receipts of your meal expenses for actual cost, you can use a standard meal allowance, which differs by travel destination.

IMPORTANT NOTES & IDEAS

Use this calendar to record business appointments, jot down mileage, and keep track of business meals and other noteworthy items you may need to reference through the year.

_____ (MONTH) _____ (YEAR)

SUNDAY	MONDAY	TUESDAY	WEDNESDAY	THURSDAY	FRIDAY	SATURDAY

Goals

Notes

MONTHLY BUSINESS INCOME & EXPENSES

Use the following table to budget and record actual expenses for your business. The items listed below are the common expenses found on business tax forms. At years end, calculate the totals and hand to your accountant (with receipts for back up of course).

INCOME	PROJECTED	ACTUAL
MONTH #1		

EXPENSES	PROJECTED	ACTUAL
ADVERTISING		
CAR & TRUCK		
COMMISSIONS & FEES		
CONTRACT LABOR		
DEPLETION		
DEPRECIATION		
EMPLOYEE BENEFIT PLANS		
INSURANCE		
MORTGAGE		
LEGAL & PROFESSIONAL FEES		
OFFICE EXPENSES RENSIONS		
RENT OR LEASE (VEHICLES)		
RENT OR LEASE (OTHER BUSINESS PROPERTY)		
REPAIRS & MAINTENANCE		
SUPPLIES		
TAXES & LICENSES		
TRAVEL		
MEALS & ENTERTAINMENT		
UTILITIES		
WAGES		
OTHER EXPENSES		
TOTAL		

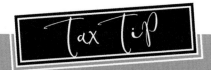

GIFTS

You can deduct the cost of gifts given to customers or employees. However, the deduction for gifts is limited to $25 per person.

IMPORTANT NOTES & IDEAS

Use this calendar to record business appointments, jot down mileage, and keep track of business meals and other noteworthy items you may need to reference through the year.

———— (MONTH) ———— ———— (YEAR) ————

SUNDAY	MONDAY	TUESDAY	WEDNESDAY	THURSDAY	FRIDAY	SATURDAY

Notes

Goals

MONTHLY BUSINESS INCOME & EXPENSES

Use the following table to budget and record actual expenses for your business. The items listed below are the common expenses found on business tax forms. At years end, calculate the totals and hand to your accountant (with receipts for back up of course).

INCOME	PROJECTED	ACTUAL
MONTH #1		

EXPENSES	PROJECTED	ACTUAL
ADVERTISING		
CAR & TRUCK		
COMMISSIONS & FEES		
CONTRACT LABOR		
DEPLETION		
DEPRECIATION		
EMPLOYEE BENEFIT PLANS		
INSURANCE		
MORTGAGE		
LEGAL & PROFESSIONAL FEES		
OFFICE EXPENSES RENSIONS		
RENT OR LEASE (VEHICLES)		
RENT OR LEASE (OTHER BUSINESS PROPERTY)		
REPAIRS & MAINTENANCE		
SUPPLIES		
TAXES & LICENSES		
TRAVEL		
MEALS & ENTERTAINMENT		
UTILITIES		
WAGES		
OTHER EXPENSES		
TOTAL		

RECORD KEEPING

Keep your records for 3 years (if you have filed your return). If you have not filed your return, not reported all of your income, or filed a fraudulent return, keep your records *indefinitely*.

IMPORTANT NOTES & IDEAS

Use this calendar to record business appointments, jot down mileage, and keep track of business meals and other noteworthy items you may need to reference through the year.

_____ (MONTH)   _____ (YEAR)

SUNDAY	MONDAY	TUESDAY	WEDNESDAY	THURSDAY	FRIDAY	SATURDAY

Notes

Goals

MONTHLY BUSINESS INCOME & EXPENSES

Use the following table to budget and record actual expenses for your business. The items listed below are the common expenses found on business tax forms. At years end, calculate the totals and hand to your accountant (with receipts for back up of course).

INCOME	PROJECTED	ACTUAL
MONTH #1		

EXPENSES	PROJECTED	ACTUAL
ADVERTISING		
CAR & TRUCK		
COMMISSIONS & FEES		
CONTRACT LABOR		
DEPLETION		
DEPRECIATION		
EMPLOYEE BENEFIT PLANS		
INSURANCE		
MORTGAGE		
LEGAL & PROFESSIONAL FEES		
OFFICE EXPENSES RENSIONS		
RENT OR LEASE (VEHICLES)		
RENT OR LEASE (OTHER BUSINESS PROPERTY)		
REPAIRS & MAINTENANCE		
SUPPLIES		
TAXES & LICENSES		
TRAVEL		
MEALS & ENTERTAINMENT		
UTILITIES		
WAGES		
OTHER EXPENSES		
TOTAL		

QUARTER 4 GOALS

Use this sheet to plan goals for the quarter. Whether its launching a new product or improving the way you do business, whatever your goals are for the quarter, jot them down here and check them off when you have accomplished the goal. Simple!

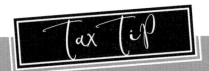

CHOOSING A PREPARER

Ask as many questions as you need to feel comfortable. Remember, YOU are ultimately responsible for what is on your return once it is filed. If you don't feel comfortable, take your business elsewhere.

IMPORTANT NOTES & IDEAS

Use this calendar to record business appointments, jot down mileage, and keep track of business meals and other noteworthy items you may need to reference through the year.

(MONTH) _____   (YEAR) _____

SUNDAY	MONDAY	TUESDAY	WEDNESDAY	THURSDAY	FRIDAY	SATURDAY

Notes

Goals

MONTHLY BUSINESS INCOME & EXPENSES

Use the following table to budget and record actual expenses for your business. The items listed below are the common expenses found on business tax forms. At years end, calculate the totals and hand to your accountant (with receipts for back up of course).

INCOME	PROJECTED	ACTUAL
MONTH #1		

EXPENSES	PROJECTED	ACTUAL
ADVERTISING		
CAR & TRUCK		
COMMISSIONS & FEES		
CONTRACT LABOR		
DEPLETION		
DEPRECIATION		
EMPLOYEE BENEFIT PLANS		
INSURANCE		
MORTGAGE		
LEGAL & PROFESSIONAL FEES		
OFFICE EXPENSES RENSIONS		
RENT OR LEASE (VEHICLES)		
RENT OR LEASE (OTHER BUSINESS PROPERTY)		
REPAIRS & MAINTENANCE		
SUPPLIES		
TAXES & LICENSES		
TRAVEL		
MEALS & ENTERTAINMENT		
UTILITIES		
WAGES		
OTHER EXPENSES		
TOTAL		

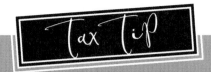

INVENTORY

If you are a small business that sells merchandise, you can use the cash method of accounting.

You are a qualifying small business taxpayer if your average annual gross receipts are more than $1 million but less than $10 million.

You may also deduct the inventory as materials and supplies instead (if those items are NOT incidental).

** Other rules apply. See **Publication 334** for more information.*

IMPORTANT NOTES & IDEAS

Use this calendar to record business appointments, jot down mileage, and keep track of business meals and other noteworthy items you may need to reference through the year.

(MONTH) _____ (YEAR) _____

SUNDAY	MONDAY	TUESDAY	WEDNESDAY	THURSDAY	FRIDAY	SATURDAY

Notes

Goals

MONTHLY BUSINESS INCOME & EXPENSES

Use the following table to budget and record actual expenses for your business. The items listed below are the common expenses found on business tax forms. At years end, calculate the totals and hand to your accountant (with receipts for back up of course).

INCOME	PROJECTED	ACTUAL
MONTH #1		

EXPENSES	PROJECTED	ACTUAL
ADVERTISING		
CAR & TRUCK		
COMMISSIONS & FEES		
CONTRACT LABOR		
DEPLETION		
DEPRECIATION		
EMPLOYEE BENEFIT PLANS		
INSURANCE		
MORTGAGE		
LEGAL & PROFESSIONAL FEES		
OFFICE EXPENSES RENSIONS		
RENT OR LEASE (VEHICLES)		
RENT OR LEASE (OTHER BUSINESS PROPERTY)		
REPAIRS & MAINTENANCE		
SUPPLIES		
TAXES & LICENSES		
TRAVEL		
MEALS & ENTERTAINMENT		
UTILITIES		
WAGES		
OTHER EXPENSES		
TOTAL		

TRAVEL

Travel expenses for conventions are deductible if you can show that your attendance benefits your trade or business. Be sure to keep those brochures or pamphlets (or a scanned copy).

IMPORTANT NOTES & IDEAS

Use this calendar to record business appointments, jot down mileage, and keep track of business meals and other noteworthy items you may need to reference through the year.

(MONTH) _____ (YEAR) _____

SUNDAY	MONDAY	TUESDAY	WEDNESDAY	THURSDAY	FRIDAY	SATURDAY

Notes

Goals

MONTHLY BUSINESS INCOME & EXPENSES

Use the following table to budget and record actual expenses for your business. The items listed below are the common expenses found on business tax forms. At years end, calculate the totals and hand to your accountant (with receipts for back up of course).

INCOME	PROJECTED	ACTUAL
MONTH #1		

EXPENSES	PROJECTED	ACTUAL
ADVERTISING		
CAR & TRUCK		
COMMISSIONS & FEES		
CONTRACT LABOR		
DEPLETION		
DEPRECIATION		
EMPLOYEE BENEFIT PLANS		
INSURANCE		
MORTGAGE		
LEGAL & PROFESSIONAL FEES		
OFFICE EXPENSES RENSIONS		
RENT OR LEASE (VEHICLES)		
RENT OR LEASE (OTHER BUSINESS PROPERTY)		
REPAIRS & MAINTENANCE		
SUPPLIES		
TAXES & LICENSES		
TRAVEL		
MEALS & ENTERTAINMENT		
UTILITIES		
WAGES		
OTHER EXPENSES		
TOTAL		

45330786R00033

Made in the USA
Middletown, DE
30 June 2017